Autumn
Publishing

Published in 2023
First published in the UK by Autumn Publishing
An imprint of Igloo Books Ltd
Cottage Farm, NN6 0BJ, UK
Owned by Bonnier Books
Sveavägen 56, Stockholm, Sweden
www.igloobooks.com

0423 002
4 6 8 10 9 7 5 3
ISBN 978-1-78810-841-6

Printed and manufactured in China

DISNEY · PIXAR
MY MEGA BOOK OF FUN

CONTENTS

Autumn
Publishing

The Story of the Film

Dory was a little blue tang who lived with her parents. From a very young age, Dory had a lot of trouble remembering things.

"Hi, I'm Dory," she would say. Then she would explain that she had short-term memory loss.

Dory's mum and dad did everything they could to stop her from getting lost. But one day, Dory wandered off and couldn't find her way back!

Years later, Dory asked her friends Marlin and Nemo to travel across the ocean with her to find her parents. They hitched a ride to California with their old friend, Crush the turtle, and soon arrived in Morro Bay, ready to start their search.

Just then, Dory was scooped up by a human and carried away in a boat. There was nothing Marlin and Nemo could do.

Suddenly, a voice came over a loudspeaker in the distance: "Welcome to the Marine Life Institute, where we believe in Rescue, Rehabilitation and Release."

The next thing Dory knew, she had a tag clipped to her fin and was dropped into a tank.

Suddenly, an octopus appeared. He reached one of his long tentacles towards Dory. "Name's Hank," he said.

Hank explained that Dory was in Quarantine and the tag on her fin was a transport tag – it meant she was going to be taken to an aquarium in Cleveland.

"Cleveland!" gasped Dory. "No, I can't go to the Cleveland! I have to get to the Jewel of Morro Bay, California…"

"That's this place," said Hank. "The Marine Life Institute. The JEWEL of Morro Bay, California. You're here."

Hank said he would help Dory search for her parents if she gave him her transport tag. He liked the idea of living in a nice, safe tank in Cleveland – he didn't want to be sent back to the ocean. Dory agreed to the deal, so Hank scooped her up into a coffee pot full of cold water and they set off to the tank where Dory hoped to find her parents.

Hank helped Dory to the tank and she swam down through the clear, cool water. At the bottom, she saw a trail of shells and followed it. She suddenly recognised the trail – she'd seen it when she was a child.

Dory gasped. This was her home! Her parents had made the shell path to guide her back whenever she got lost.

Just then, Dory noticed an entrance to a pipe. She remembered that her parents had warned her not to go near it, as the strong current it caused would carry her away. Young Dory had forgotten and been sucked into the pipe!

"It was my fault," Dory whispered. "My parents… I lost them."

Dory swam in circles, not sure what to do next! A friendly crab spoke to her and explained that all the blue tangs had been taken to Quarantine, ready to be shipped to the aquarium in Cleveland.

Dory couldn't believe it!

The only way back to Quarantine was through the pipes, so Dory nervously swam in... and was soon lost.

But suddenly, two shapes emerged from the darkness. Marlin and Nemo had found her! They had met a bird called Becky, who carried them in a bucket into the Marine Life Institute to search for Dory.

Dory was thrilled! She explained everything and the three of them found the way together.

When Marlin, Nemo and Dory reached Quarantine, the tank of blue tangs had already been loaded on the truck to Cleveland!

Luckily, Hank was there. He lifted Dory and her friends into a coffee pot filled with water and put them into the tank on the truck.

The other blue tangs recognised Dory, but they had sad news. Dory's parents had been sent to Quarantine years ago and nobody knew what had happened to them.

Dory was heartbroken. She drifted slowly into the waiting coffee pot, but suddenly it fell over and smashed! Dory fell in the drain and back to the ocean.

Alone again, Dory swam through the water out in the bay,
wondering what she should do. Then, something caught her eye –
it was a shell trail. Dory liked shells, so she followed the trail.
Suddenly, two blue tangs appeared. Dory gasped. Her parents!
Dory's parents had been creating shell pathways all this time,
in the hope that Dory would see them and remember.

"It's you! It's really you!" cried Dory as she burst into tears.

"Oh, honey, you found us," said Dory's mum. "And you know why you found us? Because you remembered. You remembered in your own amazing Dory way."

Dory was so happy, but she hadn't forgotten her other family, Marlin and Nemo. She had to save them!

With help from her new friends, Dory caught up with the truck that was carrying Marlin, Nemo and Hank, and forced it to stop on a bridge. Destiny, a whale shark from the Marine Life Institute, used her tail to flip Dory up to the truck and then Hank helped her into the tank with her friends.

Nemo was touched to see Dory. "Dory! You came back!"

Dory smiled. "Of course. I couldn't leave my family."

Marlin called for Becky to come and get them. Becky arrived, but only scooped up Marlin and Nemo. She left Dory behind!

Marlin, Nemo and Dory's parents watched as the driver closed the truck doors and drove away. Dory and Hank were trapped!

Back on the truck, Hank slid through a vent in the roof and down onto the windscreen. The shocked driver pulled over and jumped out. Hank slid inside, locked the doors and started to drive.

"Hank," said Dory. "I'm going to ask you to do something crazy."

Dory's family watched in amazement as Hank drove the truck straight off the bridge – and into the ocean! The doors flew open and all the fish spilled out into the sea. They were free!

Dory returned to life on the reef. Her whole blue tang family and all her new friends joined her. She was happier than she had ever been!

But Marlin was nervous that Dory would get lost again and often followed her. One day, Marlin caught up with Dory and they bobbed in the water at the edge of the reef, gazing out into the blue ocean.

"Wow. It really is quite a view," said Marlin.

"Yup," replied Dory.

Dory turned round to look towards her home and saw an even better sight – her whole family, together again.

"Unforgettable," she said.

The Story of
the Film

When Andy was young, his toys enjoyed exciting adventures every day. Being played with – and being loved – by a kid was the best feeling in the whole world for a toy.

As the years went by, Andy played less with his toys and soon he would be going to college. That meant playtime was over for the gang – maybe forever!

COLLEGE

Before Andy left home, he put some of the toys into one of the bin bags his mum had given him. Andy picked up his two favourite toys, Woody and Buzz. He paused, then put Woody into a box marked 'College' and Buzz into the bin bag.

Woody and Buzz were shocked!
Was Andy REALLY going to throw out the toys he had always loved so much?

Woody soon realised that Andy meant to store the toys in the attic for safekeeping. But Woody watched in horror as Andy's mum mistook the bag for rubbish – she took it outside to be collected by the rubbish truck!

Woody sneaked outside and tried to explain to the other toys what had happened, but they wouldn't believe him.

"Andy threw us out!" cried Slinky Dog.

Woody's friends decided to climb into a box bound for the Sunnyside Daycare centre, which they had spotted in the boot of Andy's mum's car. Woody had no choice but to go along with them.

When the car pulled up in front of Sunnyside Daycare, everyone, except Woody, was excited to see the children playing outside. And the daycare toys seemed cheerful and friendly too.

"Welcome to Sunnyside, folks!" called Lots-o'-Huggin' Bear, a pink bear who smelled of strawberries. Lotso showed Buzz and the gang their new home, the Caterpillar Room.

Andy's toys couldn't wait to make Sunnyside Daycare their new home, but Woody reminded them that they still belonged to Andy.

"We can have a new life here, Woody," Jessie argued. Why would they want to go somewhere they weren't wanted?

Sadly, Woody left his friends. He managed to escape onto the roof of Sunnyside, where he found an old kite. He used it to fly out beyond the daycare centre's walls.

Suddenly, a gust of wind carried the cowboy into a tree. *WHOOSH!*

Bonnie, a little girl who attended Sunnyside, found Woody dangling upside down in the branches and put him in her rucksack.

How would Woody find his way back to Andy now?

Meanwhile, at Sunnyside Daycare, Andy's toys couldn't wait to be played with by the children in the Caterpillar Room... but it wasn't what the toys expected at all!

Excited toddlers tangled Slinky's coil, broke off Rex's tail and used Buzz as a hammer! *BASH!*

"I see Andy!" Mrs Potato Head suddenly gasped. She had left one of her eyes back in Andy's room. "Andy's looking for us!" she continued. "I think he did mean to put us in the attic and not throw us out!"

Suddenly, the other toys realised Woody was right after all!

After watching a group of older kids play gently with Lotso and the other daycare toys in the Butterfly Room, Buzz decided to talk to Lotso.

The pink bear wanted Buzz – and only Buzz – to join the Butterfly Room. When Buzz refused to abandon his friends, Lotso switched him back to his original factory settings. Buzz thought he was a real Space Ranger again!

Lotso asked Buzz to watch over Andy's other toys like prisoners.

Buzz did as he was told because he had forgotten they were his friends!

In Bonnie's bedroom, Woody met her toys. He soon discovered that Lotso and his accomplice, Big Baby, had once belonged to a little girl called Daisy. Daisy had accidentally lost the two toys during a trip and her parents had given her replacements.

Lotso had never forgiven Daisy for replacing him. He was mean and bitter, and now he ruled over Sunnyside Daycare! After hearing this, Woody immediately returned to Sunnyside Daycare to help his friends to escape.

Together, the gang rescued Buzz and escaped through a rubbish chute. But just as they were nearly free, they were stopped by Lotso!

Woody reminded Lotso about Daisy, but it was too late for the pink bear to change his ways. Suddenly, a lorry picked up the bin and tipped out the toys at the rubbish dump!

Lotso got trapped in a churning tide of rubbish. Woody and Buzz quickly rescued him. But Andy's toys ended up on a conveyor belt and they were heading for a fiery furnace! Lotso didn't take his chance to save the rest of the toys!

As they were carried towards the furnace, Andy's toys thought it was the end…

But just then, a huge claw appeared above them. The Aliens were controlling the crane! They scooped up all of the toys and carried them to safety.

The toys hitched a ride back to Andy's house on a lorry. Lotso found his way on to a lorry too… a bin man had strapped him to the front grill and he would not be getting off anytime soon!

Back at Andy's, the toys jumped into a box and Woody wrote a note on the outside. The note had Bonnie's address on it. Andy found the note and gave his old toys to Bonnie. He knew she would take good care of them.

"Bye guys," Andy said, taking one last look at his toys.

Woody and Buzz watched Andy drive away.

"So long, partner," Woody said.

Buzz put his arm round Woody. Their life with Andy was ending, but their adventures with Bonnie had only just begun.

Awesome Activities and Colouring

The Good Dinosaur

Meet Poppa, an Apatosaurus.
He is a farmer on Clawtooth Mountain.

Momma and Poppa decide to start a family. They look on, excited and proud, as an egg is about to hatch.

Out hatches little Arlo!
He may be small, but he's happy.

The family have made their marks on
the silo for storing food – all except Arlo.

He knows he'll have
to do something big
to earn his mark, but
he's not sure what.

One night, Poppa takes Arlo to a field. A firefly lands on Arlo's nose and frightens him, but then Poppa gently blows on a firefly and it starts to glow. Arlo feels safe.

The next day, Poppa gives Arlo a very important task – catching the critters who steal food from the silo. But when Arlo sees a critter, he yells in fright and scares it away.

Poppa leads Arlo over the fence to help him find the critter. The pair get caught up in a violent storm. Poppa pushes Arlo to safety, but then Poppa gets swept away in a flood.

With Poppa no longer around, the family
work twice as hard. Arlo is desperate to help.

But the family's hard work is for nothing – this cute-looking critter keeps on breaking into the silo and eating their crops!

One day, the little critter sees Arlo patrolling round the silo.
The critter jumps onto Arlo's snout.

Arlo is scared of the critter. As Arlo runs away,
he trips and falls into a river!

Soon, Arlo is washed up on dry land. He climbs
to the top of a hill and looks down at the valley.
"I can… I can follow the river home!" Arlo realises.

After walking for a long time, Arlo slips and falls
and his foot gets stuck between some rocks.
He curls up for the night and falls fast asleep.

When Arlo wakes up, his foot is now free! He spies some footprints in the ground – the little critter must have helped him. Soon, it starts to rain. The little dinosaur decides to build a shelter.

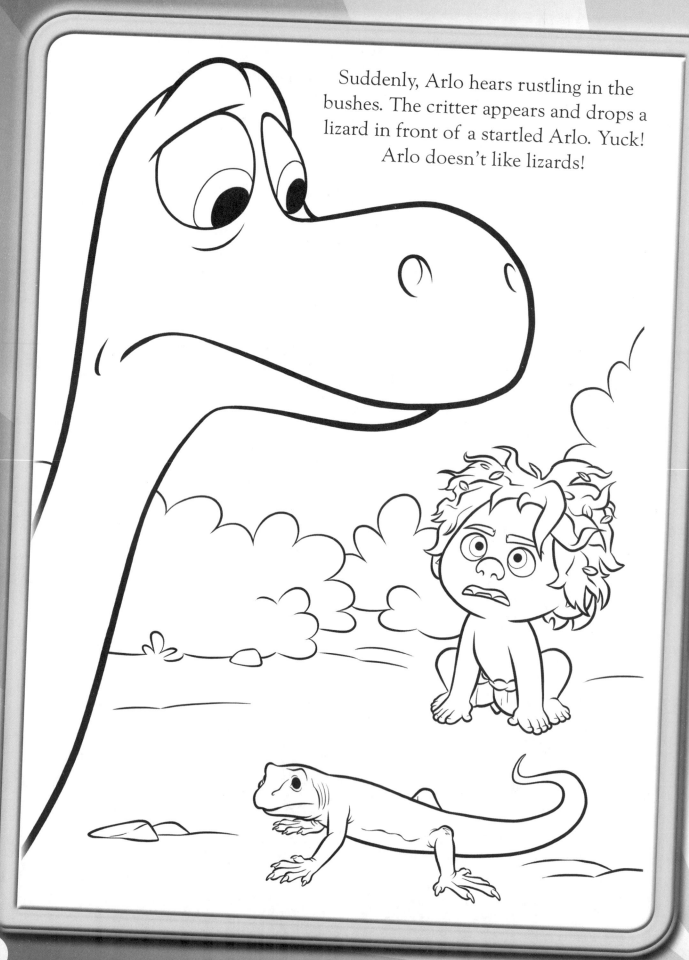

Suddenly, Arlo hears rustling in the bushes. The critter appears and drops a lizard in front of a startled Arlo. Yuck! Arlo doesn't like lizards!

The critter runs off and soon brings Arlo some delicious berries.
The pair sit down together and munch away happily.

The next day, Arlo and the critter meet
a strange dinosaur named Pet Collector.

Pet Collector likes the critter and challenges Arlo to a naming contest: whoever names the critter gets to keep him. "Spot!" says Arlo. The critter looks up. Arlo has won!

At night, hundreds of fireflies light up the sky.
Spot is amazed. Arlo shows him how to play with them.

Arlo and Spot use twigs to tell each other about their families. They howl into the night.

The next morning, they hear thunder in the distance.
A storm is coming. Arlo and Spot run into
a forest and hide under a tree root.

After the storm has died down, Pterodactyls dive out of the sky.
They want to steal Spot! Arlo picks up Spot and runs away.

As they escape the flying dinosaurs, Arlo and Spot run into three friendly T. rexes. The T. rexes tell Arlo and Spot that they have lost their herd of longhorns.

Arlo knows that Spot can sniff out anything – so he's sure that Spot can help find the longhorns. Suddenly, the group see some mean-looking raptors. Raptors steal longhorns.

Butch has an idea: Arlo can help them catch the raptors by acting as bait. He tries screaming to attract the raptors... but nothing comes out! Spot knows what to do – he bites Arlo, who lets out a huge yell!

The T. rexes fight off the vicious raptors and their herd is safe.
The next day, Spot and Arlo continue on their journey.

At the top of a hill, Arlo pops his head through the clouds.
What a view! In the distance, they see Clawtooth Mountain.

Suddenly, clouds start to gather and lightning flashes.
A group of Pterodactyls appears in the sky.

Just then, a Pterodactyl swoops down and captures Spot.
Arlo rescues Spot by throwing a tree trunk
at the Pterodactyl to scare him away.

By the next morning, Spot and Arlo have nearly reached Clawtooth Mountain. Suddenly, a human family appears out of the woods.

The humans want to be Spot's new family. Spot and Arlo hug and say goodbye. They will miss each other, but will never forget the adventure they had together.

Soon after, Arlo finally sees his family's farm. He's made it and he is no longer the dinosaur he used to be.

Momma is so happy to have Arlo back home. He has proven his bravery. At last, Arlo can add his mark to the family silo.

Riley's first day of school is not going well. Look carefully at the following picture for one minute, then cover it with a piece of paper and answer the questions.

1. How many of Riley's new classmates are in the scene? ....

2. What is on the wall at the back of the classroom?

....

3. How many students are wearing glasses? ....

4. What is Riley wearing? ....

5. What is on Riley's desk? ....

Answers on page 162

Can you find the shadow that exactly matches
the big picture of Joy and Sadness?

a

b

c

d

Answer on page 162

Fear's job is to keep Riley safe.

When Riley was little, she had an imaginary friend named Bing Bong who cried sweets. Draw a new character to play with Bing Bong in the space below.

Broccoli on pizza? Things are strange in San Francisco! Draw a new pizza in this box with all your favourite toppings.

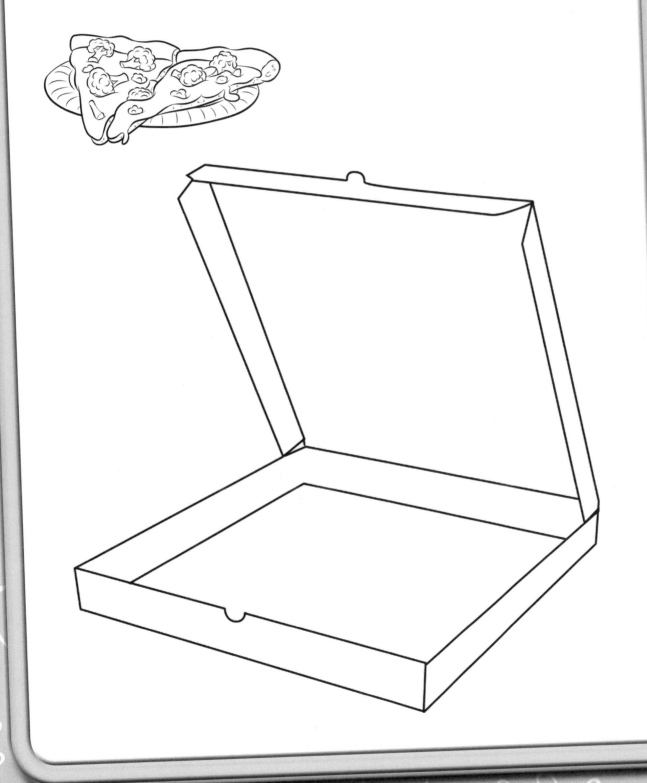

Uh-oh! Bing Bong must have been crying sweets again!
How many sweets can you find in the scene below?
Now, colour in the picture.

Number of sweets:

Only one of these shadows exactly matches Anger.
Circle the correct shadow.

a

b

c

d

Answer on page 162

Read the story and decide which
picture represents each missing word.
Write the correct number in each box.

Riley learned to play ☐ when she was

really little. ☐ was nervous that Riley

would fall, but ☐ was so happy to see

Riley score her first ☐ !

1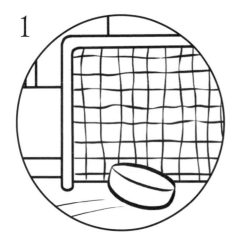

2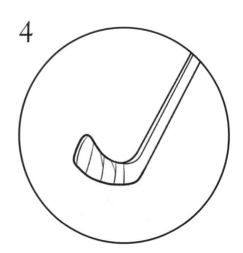

3

4

Answers on page 162

Imagination Land is Bing Bong's favourite place in Riley's mind. Use your colours and your own imagination to finish this picture!

Hurry! Joy and Sadness need to board the Train of Thought so they can get back to Headquarters and help Riley. Which path will take them to the train?

Answer on page 162

Joy and Bing Bong have met in Long Term Memory.
Draw lines to connect each missing piece
to the correct space in the picture.

① ② ③

a

b

c

d

e

④ ⑤

Answers on page 162

What does Riley need to play her favourite sport?
Join the dots to show what it is, then write
your answer below.

_ _ _ _ _ _ _ _ _

_ _ _ _ _

Answer on page 162

Draw a line from each feeling
to the matching Emotion

a

b

c

d

e

1. furious

2. happy

3. gross

4. forlorn

5. scared

6. glum

7. mad

8. jolly

9. unhappy

10. afraid

11. livid

12. revolting

13. cheerful

14. nervous

15. repulsive

Answers on page 162

Use the grid as a guide to copy this picture of
Joy, square by square, into the empty grid below.
Then, colour her in!

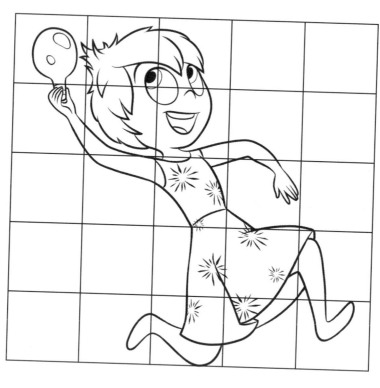

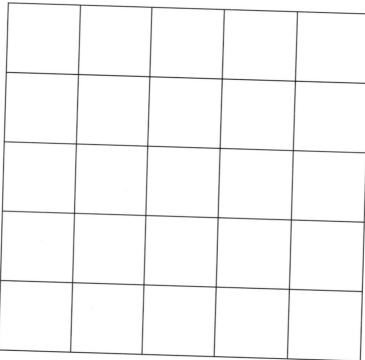

Rainbow Unicorn is the star of Riley's best dreams. Use all the colours of the rainbow to colour her in!

Joy and Sadness are two of Riley's Emotions.

Make this picture of Bing Bong as colourful as you can.

Complete the story below by writing down what you think the characters are saying to each other. What is the name of your story?

TITLE: _____

Joy and Sadness can't find Bing Bong!
Lead the two Emotions through the maze below
to reunite them with Riley's imaginary friend.

START

FINISH

Answer on page 162

Riley's Emotions make a great team. They work together to make sure that Riley has the best life ever. Add colour to this picture.

Joy and Sadness are totally different from each other, just like the words below. Draw lines to connect each word on the left to its opposite on the right.

loud

even

dark

inside

best

always

begin

day

first

high

fast

never

worst

slow

end

quiet

odd

last

light

low

night

outside

Answers on page 162

Riley and her parents have arrived at their new house and they're playing hockey in the living room! Can you spot and circle eight things that have changed in the second picture?

Answers on page 162

Disgust keeps Riley away from all things gross.
Can you colour her in?

Joy and Sadness have been sucked out of Headquarters and Fear is freaking out! Find the picture of Fear that matches the big picture of him.

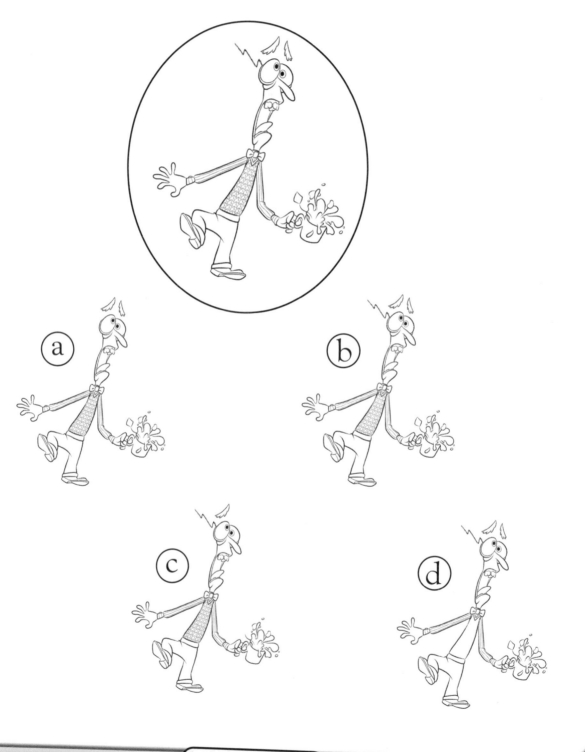

Answer on page 162

Riley has found out that the removal van is late and none of her things have arrived from her old home. Help to cheer her up and decorate her new room for her.

Anger gets so steamed up that fire and smoke
come out of his head! Colour him in.

Meet Dory, a blue tang fish.
She has short-term memory loss.

Jenny and Charlie are Dory's parents. They love Dory very much, but sometimes they worry about her.

One day, Dory gets lost. But she eventually forgets that she is lost and grows up to be a happy, friendly fish.

Dory meets a clownfish named Marlin.
He is looking for his son, Nemo. Nemo is lost, too!

The two fish go on an adventure across the ocean to find Nemo. Soon, Marlin, Nemo and Dory become just like family.

One day, Dory finally remembers her parents.
She asks Marlin and Nemo to help her find them.

Crush, Marlin and Dory's sea turtle friend, gives them
a ride to Dory's home – the Jewel of Morro Bay, California.

When they arrive, Dory gets stuck in some plastic rings.
Suddenly, a large hand plunges into the water and grabs her!

The Jewel of Morro Bay is the Marine Life
Institute – the MLI. Dory is given a tag, which
means she will be moved to Cleveland.

Dory meets an octopus named Hank.
He wants to go to Cleveland, so he agrees to help
Dory find her parents in exchange for her tag.

Dory leaps inside a bucket and gets carried to another tank.

Destiny is a whale shark – and she remembers Dory.
They used to speak whale to each other through the pipes.

Bailey, a beluga whale, lives next door to Destiny. He's sick, so he can't use his special echolocation skill to see things that are far away.

Bailey and Destiny know where Dory's parents live!
They tell her to go to an area of the MLI called Open Ocean.

Meanwhile, a loon named Becky flies Marlin and Nemo towards the MLI. They're going to rescue Dory!

On their way to Open Ocean, Hank and Dory fall into a touch pool! They try to hide from prodding hands.

Finally, Hank and Dory are safe. In the distance, Dory spots a sign for Open Ocean. "Home!" she sighs with relief.

Hank swings above Open Ocean, ready to drop Dory in.
Dory gives her tag to Hank and says goodbye.

Inside Open Ocean, Dory finds a trail of shells.
She follows them one by one until she finds...

... her home! But Dory's parents aren't there. They've been taken to Quarantine – ready to be shipped to Cleveland!

Destiny and Bailey help Dory find her way through the pipes to Quarantine. Bailey's echolocation does work after all!

Suddenly, Dory bumps into two familiar fish...
Marlin and Nemo! They make their way to
Quarantine, where they find Hank.

Hank carries Dory and drops her into a tank of blue tangs so she can look for her parents, but she can't find them.

Hank lifts Dory out of the tank, but then he gets startled by a human and drops Dory! She flies through the air and falls down a drain that leads to the ocean.

In the ocean, Dory sees lots of shell paths. They lead
to her parents! They've been waiting for Dory all this time.

Now that she's found her parents, Dory needs to rescue Marlin and Nemo. Bailey uses his echolocation to help find them.

Hank and Dory find Marlin and Nemo
in a truck heading to Cleveland.

Becky arrives to help carry the fish to safety, but Dory gets left behind!

Hank distracts the truck driver and then jumps
into the front seat with Dory. Hank steers and works
the pedals, while Dory tells him which way to go.

Dory and Hank follow the seagulls and drive
all the way into the ocean. They're free!

Back in the ocean, Dory is reunited with Marlin, Nemo and her parents. They all laugh and play together as one big, happy family.

Watch out for Lotso and his gang! Twitch, Big Baby, Lotso and Chunk should each appear once in every row and column. Draw or write the name of the missing toys in the empty boxes.

Answers on page 162

The toys have a lot to learn about
who makes the rules at Sunnyside. Join the
dots to help them see who is in charge.

Buzz knows something has changed, but he's not sure what. Can you help him find the ten things that are different in the lower picture?

Answers on page 163

Clean up Andy's room! Put the toys into the boxes by drawing a line from each toy to the correct box.

4 LEGS

2 LEGS

Answers on page 163

Copy this picture of Rex into the grid below, square by square.

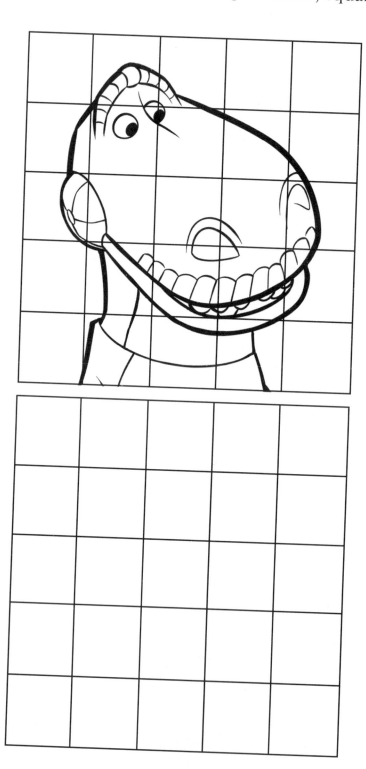

Colour this picture of the rootin' tootin' toy, Woody.

The toys have escaped from Sunnyside! Draw lines to match each set of footprints to the toy that made them.

Play this game with a friend! Choose who will be Buzz and who will be Woody, then take it in turns to fill an empty space in the grid with a drawing of your chosen character. The winner is the first player to fill three spaces in a row – in any direction!

Woody is trying to help the toys out of a rubbish bag. But something is heading their way! Connect the dots to see what it is.

Answer on page 163

Colour in Slinky, Hamm and Stretch as they play a game!

Play this game with two friends! Help the gang climb the ladders below.

1. Choose a small toy and place it on Jessie, Woody or Buzz.
2. Take it in turns to flip a coin.
3. Each time the coin lands on 'heads', you may move up one rung on your ladder. Whenever it lands on 'tails', move down one rung.
4. The first player to the top of the wall wins!

Draw lines to match the pieces to the picture. Where do they belong?

Play this game with a friend! The youngest player goes first.

- To start, the first player should draw a line connecting any two dots.
- Then, the next player draws a line. Continue taking turns.
- The lines can go across, up and down, but not diagonally.
- If the line you draw completes a square, put your initials in it.
- When all the dots are connected, count your squares. The squares with a toy inside are worth two points!
- The player with the most points wins.

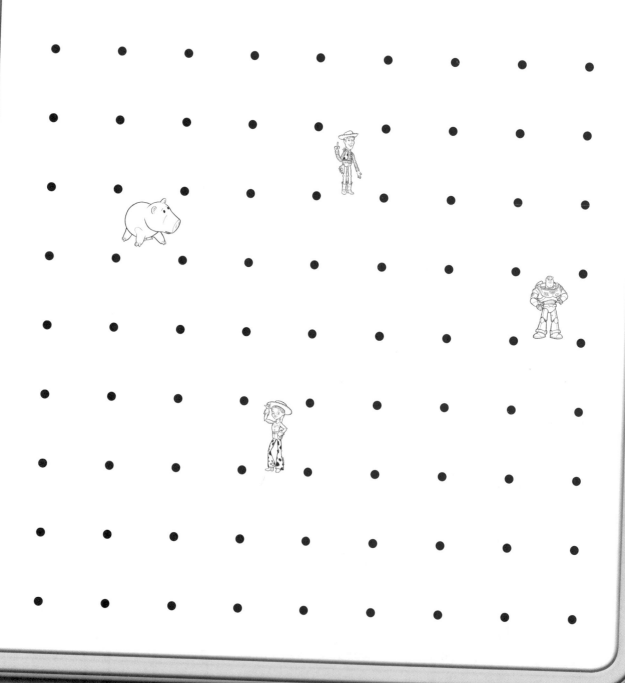

Woody and Buzz are best buddies.
Decorate them using your best pens and pencils.

What's going on in Andy's room? He thinks something has moved, but he's not sure what. Help him find ten things that have changed in the lower picture.

Answers on page 163

Each toy should appear once in each row and column.
Draw or write the name of the missing toy in each row.

Jessie, Rex and Hamm are confused by Buzz's behaviour.
Look at the comic strip. What would Jessie, Rex and Hamm say?
Write the lines, then share them with a friend or adult.

Rex is afraid that Andy will forget him. Draw a picture of Rex for Andy to take to college with him.

The toys have arrived at Sunnyside Daycare.
Look carefully at the picture for one minute. Cover the page,
then write down everything that was in the picture.
How many things did you remember?

Big Baby is trying to hide by blending in with some other baby dolls. Can you find the real Big Baby? Hint: He's the one that's different from the others.

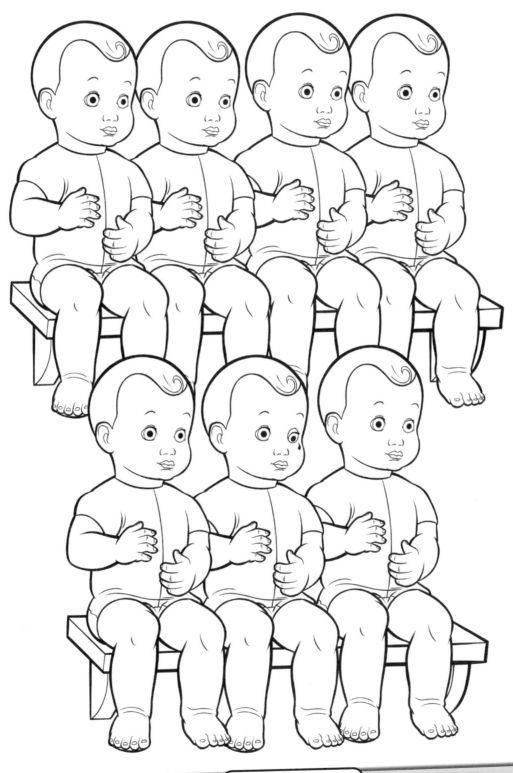

Answer on page 163

Follow these steps and use the space on the opposite page to draw Lotso.

Step 1

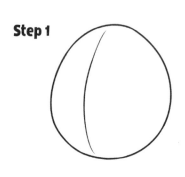

Step 2

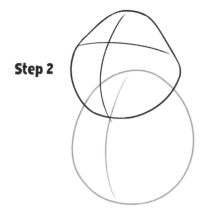

Step 3

Step 4

Now, add some detail and colour in Lotso. Don't forget to add his fur!

How many triangles can you count on Woody's kite?
Hint: There are more than 10.

Answer:

Colour these pieces, then ask an adult to cut them out along the lines. Now, see if you can complete the puzzle! There's a second one on the back.

Woody wants to find his way back to Andy.
Can you help him by finding the way through the maze?

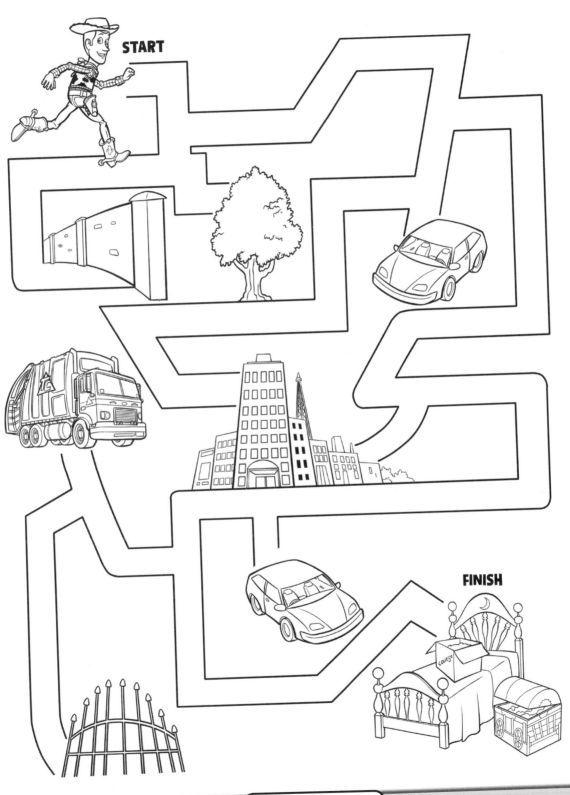

START

FINISH

Answer on page 164

Help Jessie round up Andy's toys. Circle Buzz, Woody, Hamm, three Aliens, Rex and Bullseye in this picture.

There are some things in this picture that do not belong at Sunnyside Daycare. Find the eight objects below:

- Andy's picture
- bath
- flying fish
- campfire
- knight in armour
- chandelier
- spaghetti
- dragon

Answers on page 164

It's night-time at Sunnyside. Draw a
line from each toy to its shadow.

Answers on page 164

Help the toys find each other in the rubbish dump!
Complete the patterns below by drawing the correct
item in the blank spaces in each sequence.

Look at the comic strip. What happens next?
Draw the next scene and share it with a friend or adult.

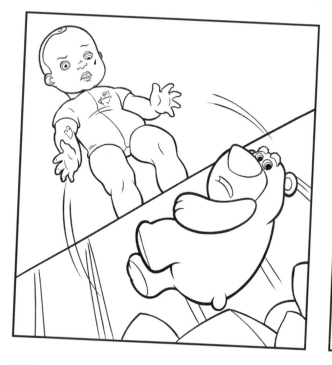

Join the dots from 1 to 10 on both sides of Buzz
to help him fly to infinity, and beyond!

Answer on page 164

Colour this picture of Jessie and Bullseye.

Woody is flying away from Sunnyside Daycare. Help him through the maze of roads back to Andy's house.

START

TRASH

FINISH

Answer on page 164

1. Look at the picture.
2. Without counting, guess how many balls are in the container. Write your guess here ____.
3. Now, count the balls. Put the number here ____.

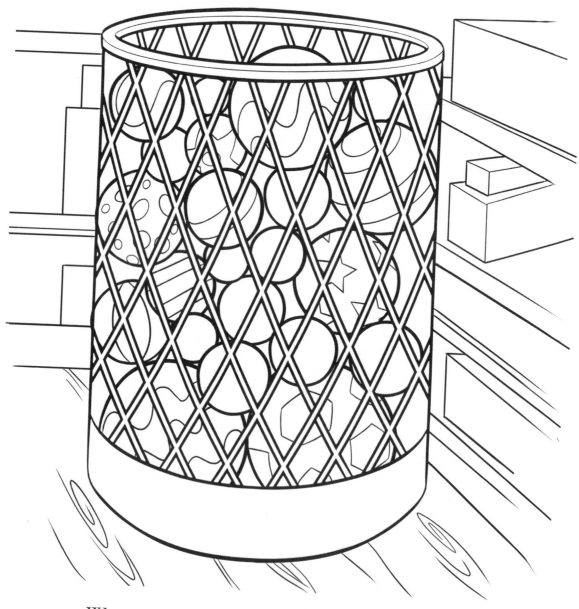

Was your guess close? Practise guessing and counting the things around you.

Answer on page 164

Buzz is ready to blast off into space!
Using your best pencils, design a brand-new spaceship for him.

Andy loved playing with his toys when he was young.

The toys will have a great new life with Bonnie.

Answers

Page 67
1. Three classmates
2. Map of the world and noticeboard
3. One student
4. Trousers and a zip-up top
5. A book, a notebook and a pen

Page 68
d is the matching shadow.

Page 72
There are 21 sweets.

Page 73
c is the matching shadow.

Page 74
The order is: 4, 2, 3, 1

Page 76
Path a will take them to the train.

Page 77
1-b, 2-d, 3-a, 4-e, 5-c

Page 78
Hockey stick

Page 79
a. Joy – 2, 8, 13
b. Disgust – 3, 12, 15
c. Anger – 1, 7, 11
d. Fear – 5, 10, 14
e. Sadness – 4, 6, 9

Page 85

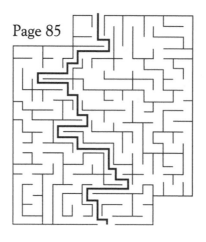

Page 87
loud/quiet
even/odd
dark/light
inside/outside
best/worst
always/never
begin/end
day/night
first/last
high/low
fast/slow

Page 88

Page 90
b is the matching picture.

Page 124
Row 1: Chunk
Row 2: Lotso
Row 3: Big Baby
Row 4: Twitch

Page 125
It's Lotso!

162

Answers

Page 126

Page 132

Page 138

Page 127
2 Legs: Woody, Jessie, Buzz and Rex
4 Legs: Bullseye and Hamm

Page 135

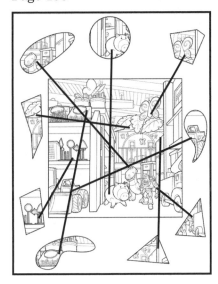

Page 139
Row 1: Jessie
Row 2: Rex
Row 3: Buzz
Row 4: Woody

Page 130

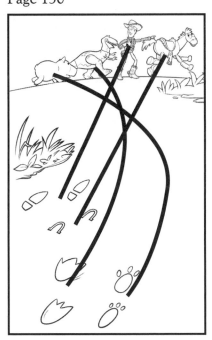

Page 143

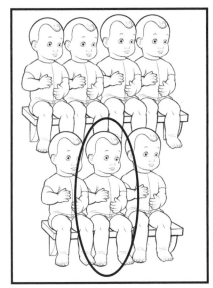

Answers

Page 146
If you found:
17 triangles: good job!
23 triangles: incredible!
25 triangles: the best!

Page 149
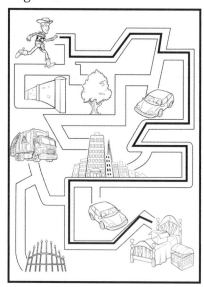

Page 150

Page 151

Page 152

Page 153

Page 155

Page 157

Page 158
There are 22 balls.

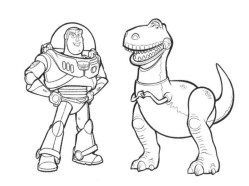

FROM THE MOVIE

Disney · PIXAR

INSIDE OUT

The Story of the Film

When a little girl called Riley was born, her first
Emotion, Joy, ran Headquarters from inside Riley's
mind. As Joy watched what happened to Riley on
a big screen, memory spheres were created.

Joy picked up the first memory – it showed Riley
as a baby. It was gold because the sphere contained
a happy memory. Joy placed the sphere on a shelf in
Headquarters.

As Riley grew older, the shelves in Headquarters became full of memory spheres. Joy was also joined by four more Emotions – Sadness, Disgust, Anger and Fear.

Together, the Five Emotions made important choices for Riley from the console inside her mind. Joy was the leader and all she wanted was for the little girl to be happy.

Fear helped keep Riley safe. He once stopped her from tripping over a power cable when she was running through the house.

Disgust kept Riley away from things that looked, smelled or tasted funny — like broccoli!

Anger cared very deeply about things being fair. All of Riley's tantrums happened when Anger was driving the console.

Finally, there was Sadness. Her role was not as obvious as Riley's other Emotions. In fact, Joy wasn't sure why Sadness was there at all.

When something important happened to Riley, a core memory was created.

Each core memory powered Riley's Islands of Personality.

There were five islands – Goofball, Friendship, Hockey, Honesty and Family.

When Riley was 11, her mum and dad announced that they were moving from their home town in Minnesota to San Francisco. The Emotions panicked! Riley had great friends and a lovely home in Minnesota.

After a long car journey, Riley and her parents arrived at their new house in San Francisco. Riley was sad that she had to move, but Joy tried to keep Riley happy by taking control of the console.

Before long, it was Riley's first day at her new school.
Joy gave each Emotion an important job to do.

Joy was determined to keep Riley happy. She carefully
drew a circle on the floor around Sadness.

"Your job today is to make sure that all of the sadness
stays inside this circle," she told Sadness.

At school, the teacher asked Riley to introduce herself. Riley shared a happy memory of playing hockey back in Minnesota. But suddenly, she became upset.

Joy saw that Sadness had left her circle and touched the hockey memory sphere, turning it blue!

In an attempt to get rid of this new sad memory, Joy turned on the memory vacuum. Joy, Sadness and all six of Riley's core memories were sucked up into the memory vacuum tube.

Joy and Sadness were dumped out in Long Term Memory. All the Islands of Personality had turned dark, since the core memories weren't in Headquarters to power them up. Joy knew they had to get the memories back to Headquarters so the Islands would work again.

But Headquarters was far away. The different parts of Riley's mind were connected by bridges. Joy collected up the five yellow core memories and both she and Sadness headed across a bridge from Long Term Memory to Goofball Island. Joy knew they would be able to cross another bridge from Goofball Island back to Headquarters.

The pair had just made it to Goofball Island when it began to crumble. It was collapsing because Riley had got angry with her parents and stopped goofing around with her dad.

Joy grabbed Sadness and made it back to Long Term Memory just before the island disappeared. Sadness realised that they could lose the other Islands of Personality, too.

Joy tried to stay positive – they would just have to make their way to another island.

But Sadness slumped to the floor in despair. So, Joy picked up one of her legs and dragged her along.

Back in Riley's bedroom, Riley was chatting to her old friend Meg on her laptop.

Meg told Riley about a new girl on the hockey team. Riley missed playing hockey with her old friends, so the news made her angry.

At Headquarters, Anger took charge of the console and flames roared out of the top of his head.

Back in Long Term Memory, Joy and Sadness heard a loud groan as Friendship Island fell into the dump.

Joy looked up to Hockey Island. "We'll just have to go the long way round," she said.

As Joy and Sadness tried to find a bridge leading to Hockey Island, they bumped into Bing Bong, Riley's old imaginary friend.

Riley and Bing Bong used to play together – they even had a rocket wagon that was powered by a song. But over the years, Riley had forgotten him.

Bing Bong told Joy that he was in Long Term Memory looking for a good memory so that he could be part of Riley's life again.

"We're on our way to Headquarters. Come with us and we'll get Riley to remember you!" said Joy.

Bing Bong gave Joy his bag to carry the core memories in and told them that it would be much quicker to catch the Train of Thought to Headquarters. Bing Bong knew how to get to the station through Imagination Land.

Once inside, Joy and Sadness were amazed! There was
a French Fry Forest, Trophy Town and Cloud Town.
    They soon reached a House of Cards, where Bing Bong
found his rocket wagon. They also found an Imaginary
Boyfriend Generator.

Meanwhile, Riley was at the try-outs for a new hockey team.

At Headquarters, Anger, Disgust and Fear tried to get Riley through it. But the Emotions couldn't find the right memory to replace the missing core hockey memory. Riley missed the puck, fell over and then stormed off.

Inside Riley's mind, Hockey Island fell to pieces and sank into the Memory Dump.

Joy, Sadness and Bing Bong watched in horror from Imagination Land.

Inside Imagination Land, some Mind Workers took Bing Bong's rocket wagon and threw it into the Memory Dump.

"No!" yelled Bing Bong. He sat on the floor and cried sweets.

Sadness sat beside Bing Bong. "I'm sorry they took your rocket wagon," she said.

After they talked about how he felt, he said, "I feel okay now."

Joy was surprised. Sadness had made Bing Bong feel better!

Joy, Sadness and Bing Bong finally made it to the train, but it soon stopped because Riley had gone to sleep.

To wake her up, Joy and Sadness found a huge, scary clown hidden in Riley's mind. They led the clown to Dream Productions, where Riley's dreams were made. The clown appeared in Riley's dream and she woke up!

The trio ran back to the train and jumped aboard just as it was about to leave.

Meanwhile, at Headquarters, Anger had decided that the best thing for Riley was to run away – back to Minnesota. He plugged an idea bulb into the console.

After the bulb was plugged into the console, the idea popped into Riley's head just as she woke up from her scary dream.

Riley needed money to buy a bus ticket to Minnesota, so she took money from her mum's purse.

Back on the Train of Thought, Joy looked out of the train carriage and saw Honesty Island fall into the deep dump.

Suddenly, the tracks underneath the train crumbled away and the train crashed into the cliffside. Everyone on the train jumped off just before it tipped into the dump below.

After the train crash, Sadness realised they could use a
tube in Long Term Memory to get back to Headquarters.
But as Joy got sucked up the tube, it broke and Joy fell deep
into the Memory Dump!

At that moment, Riley was heading to the bus station.

Down in the dump, Joy felt hopeless. She looked at
a memory of a time when Riley had been sad but her
friends had come to cheer her up. Suddenly, Joy realised
that Sadness was important – Riley's friends came to help
because she was sad!

Just then, Bing Bong appeared. The pair came up with an idea – they could use Bing Bong's rocket wagon to fly out of the Memory Dump!

They sang loudly to power the rocket, but each time they flew up they couldn't quite reach the top of the cliff.

They gave it one last try and, without Joy noticing, Bing Bong jumped out of the rocket wagon so it could leave the Memory Dump.

"Go save Riley!" he called. "Take her to the Moon for me, okay?"

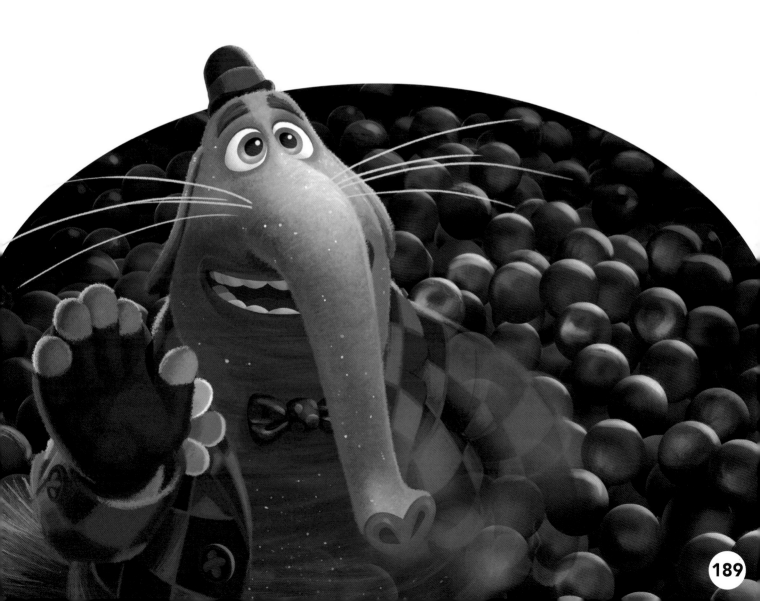

Joy spotted Sadness, who was floating on a cloud.

As Family Island crumbled away, Joy noticed an Imaginary Boyfriend and had an idea.

Joy used the Boyfriend Generator to make hundreds of boyfriends. Using them as a huge tower, she swung towards Sadness...

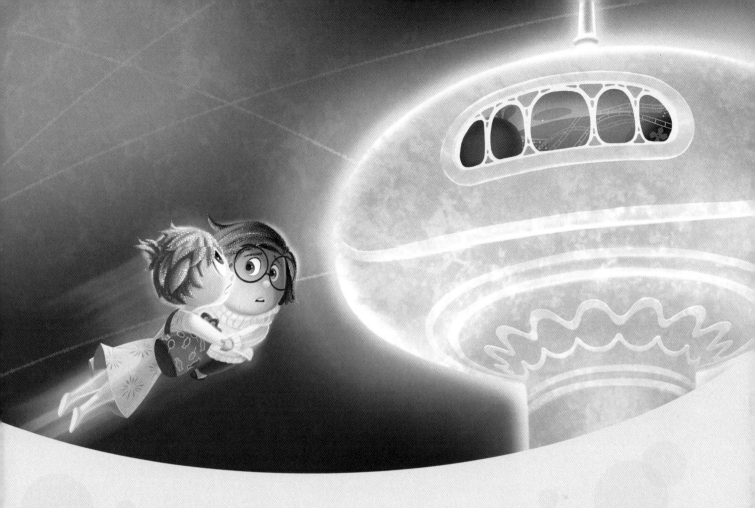

Joy grabbed hold of Sadness and the two of them flew through the air towards Headquarters. *SPLAT!* They hit the back window and started to slide down the glass.

Anger, Fear and Disgust ran towards the window. How were they going to get them inside?

Disgust had an idea! She got Anger really mad until flames burst out of him and used the fire to cut a hole in the window. Joy and Sadness climbed inside.

Joy looked up at the screen and saw that Riley was on the bus, ready to run away from home and back to Minnesota. She realised that she had to let Sadness drive and let her step up to the console.

Sadness took a deep breath and pulled out the idea bulb. On the bus, Riley suddenly felt that she had to stay. "Wait!" she called to the driver. "I want to get off!"

As the other Emotions looked on, Joy handed the core memories to Sadness and they all turned blue. Sadness placed them back in the projector that played memories on the screen in Headquarters.

Riley arrived back at her house. Her mum and dad had been worried sick. Riley told them how she missed her life back in Minnesota.

Riley, Mum and Dad hugged each other and, at Headquarters, a brand-new core memory appeared, which created a new Family Island.

A few days later, the Islands of Personality had reappeared – with a few new ones, too!

Joy, Sadness, Anger, Fear and Disgust were excited about the future. After all, Riley was 12 now... what could happen?